NEW NERD
M O N E Y

NEW NERD
MONEY

A BEGINNER'S GUIDE TO MAKING, MANAGING & GROWING MONEY

IAN MICHAEL BROCK

NEW NERD PUBLISHING

Copyright © 2024 by Ian Michael Brock.

All rights reserved. No part of this book may be used, reproduced or transmitted in any form or by any means, electronic or mechanical, including photocopying, recording or by information storage and retrieval system without written permission from the publisher, except by a reviewer who wishes to quote brief excerpts in connection with a review in a newspaper, magazine, or electronic publication.

Printed in the United States of America.

Requests for permission, for more information, or to book an event, contact publisher by sending an email :
info@newnerdpublishing.com
https://www.newnerdmoney.com

Cover photography by Sterling Gilmore

ISBN - Paperback: 979-8-9904817-0-1

The publication is designed to provide accurate and authoritative information in regard to the subject matter covered. It is sold with the understanding that the publisher is not engaged in rendering legal, accounting, or other professional services. If you require legal advice or other expert assistance, you should seek the services of a competent professional.

This is dedicated to all my mentees who tested my patience but made me a better mentor.

Who is IAN BROCK

INTRODUCTION

WHO IS IAN MICHAEL BROCK?

Cue the **James Bond** theme music . . .

When he's not acting like he's James Bond, Ian Michael Brock is the Co-Founder of Dream Hustle Code® and New Nerd. Ian is a Gen Z Powerhouse, transformational speaker, computer science activist, financial literacy & personal development coach, and author. For over 8+ years, he has been on a mission to inspire confidence in Black & Brown Youth, while empowering them with tools so that they, too, can be creators and not just be consumers. Through his journey he's done extraordinary interviews with Oprah Winfrey, Bob Johnson (Founder of BET), R. Donahue Peebles, Ben Horowitz, Steve Harvey, Dan Cathy, and Kyrie Irving to name a few.

Through his work with Dream Hustle Code, they've reached 60,000+ students virtually and in person. In 2021, he created and hosted Teen Tech LIVE, a Virtual Field Trip Event that has since hosted tens of thousands of youth all over the United States as well as Nigeria, Jamaica, Canada, London, and New Zealand.

Ian is featured in McDonald's Black & Positively Golden Mentors Commercial Campaign. Most recently, he was selected as one of McDonald's Future 22, a new campaign celebrating the work of 22 young, gifted and Black leaders. He's appeared at the BET Awards, Essence Festival of Culture, CBS Evening News, Earn Your Leisure, and he has been featured online in media outlets such as Forbes, Black Enterprise, Medium, Encyclopedia Britannica, Education Week, Thrive Global, Nike Zine, Built In Chicago, Parents, Chicago Tribune, P33, among others.

He has spoken at numerous events from Silicon Valley to Saudi Arabia including Google, Global Entrepreneurship Congress, Startup Grind Global, WE Day Chicago, The Steve Harvey Foundation Mentoring Program, the National Black MBA Association, and Essence Fest.

Most recently, Ian was named as one of the 20 individuals selected for the prestigious Thiel Fellowship Class of 2023. The Fellowship Program encourages talented young people with big ideas to start companies instead of attending college. Ian is an honoree of the 2022 Microsoft Legacy Project, being identified as one of the most influential African American community and outstanding civic leaders of our time. Ian is currently working on building a workforce development pipeline that will educate kids in financial literacy, personal development & job readiness, train them, then help to secure jobs for high school juniors and seniors who are not planning to attend college.

Outside of his work, Ian is a Board Member of WayMaker Media Inc and Rosecrans Ventures. He is an avid reader, loves to play video games and basketball, listen to music, and build and figure out mechanical products.

Scan the QR Code to connect with Ian.

AUTHOR'S MESSAGE

Being involved in all of these things, meeting all of these people and traveling to all of these cool places has allowed me to earn hundreds of thousands of dollars. Even more important are the financial strategies that I've learned along the way and how I have incorporated those strategies to grow my wealth...at 18 years old. And here's the thing, I'm not some kind of genius who just knows all of this stuff. I just started at a young age and learned how to apply the lessons from the success of others in a way that works for me. And You can do the same thing too.

By no means am I some kind of genius. The truth is, I was blessed to have two grandfathers who were both brilliant in math. My mom's father (Lolo) used his math abilities to become an electrical engineer who designed schematics for nuclear power plants. On the other hand my dad's father (Grandpa Brock) used his math skills in a very different way. He followed in the footsteps of his dad and entered the U.S. military and ironically became an Army Military Police Officer. Once he left the military, he became a truck driver and later on sold drugs as a way of making money to take care of his family and fund his dream of one day owning his own trucking company.

When I think about my two grandfathers, it's clear that both took very different paths to attaining the "American Dream." Lolo was an immigrant who migrated from the Philippines to gain a better life. Through sacrifices and being separated from his family for more than a decade, he came to America and laid the foundation for his 3 daughters to come to this country and get a better education and a better living.

They didn't come to this country super wealthy. They came, worked hard and became a middle-class family who built a respectable life in a foreign land. Money was always an issue that they worked hard to resolve. There were many things about how money, credit, and finance worked in America that they simply did not know or clearly understand.

Grandpa Brock however, grew up in America but was scarred by the impact of racism, poverty and growing up without his father in the house. He once told my dad a story of how a group of his white classmates followed him after school, tied him up to a tree, painted a white line down the back of his clothes and laughed as they called him a skunk.

One would think that growing up In America would've made it easier to achieve the so-called "American Dream." But Growing up Black in this country comes with challenges that stop many dreamers before they ever get the chance to start.

Growing up without a father in the house comes with many different challenges. There are many lessons and strategies for survival that a young man misses without his father being around to train and teach him.

When Grandpa Brock left the military and began driving a truck, he envisioned himself owning a trucking company like the one that he worked for.

When he attempted to get the financing necessary to buy his first truck, he was met with many rejections and disappointments. At the suggestion of a friend, he turned to selling drugs to survive.

I can't help but think of how the story of my grandfather's life would've played out differently if he had learned about how money, credit, and financing worked.

Would he have gotten that first truck and created a successful business? Who knows. Grandpa Brock died before I was born and I never got a chance to meet him but I bet he would've told me that the information could've changed his life.

Thinking about the journeys and choices of both of my grandfathers has inspired me to learn as much as I possibly can about wealth, how to get it and how to grow it.

Seeing how having access to this information would have changed my grandfathers' lives and their loved ones' lives for generations is what drives me to want to share this information.

> "You may not come from a wealthy family, but a wealthy family can come from you."
>
> - AUTHOR UNKNOWN

ACKNOWLEDGMENTS

I want to thank everyone who was part of the process of making this book.

Everyone that taught me valuable lessons that have made me the person that I am today.

I want to thank my supporters who have been part of the journey, especially my parents.

Mom and Dad, you are the reason that this book happened because you were my first teachers. You guided me on this journey teaching me all the skills that I needed to be successful especially in this space.

Most of all, I want to thank GOD. Without his mercy, grace and favor, without him blessing me, I wouldn't be here to tell these stories and to share this information.

Thank you to all who played a crucial role in my life and the development of this book!

CONTENTS

INTRODUCTION	vii
AUTHOR'S MESSAGE	xi
ACKNOWLEDGEMENTS	xv
CHAPTER 1 The Power of Your Thoughts	1
CHAPTER 2 It Takes Money to Make Money	11
CHAPTER 3 Financial Literacy Basics	25
CHAPTER 4 Budgeting Your Money	33

CHAPTER 5 | **45**
Understanding Credit - Part I

CHAPTER 6 | **53**
Understanding Credit - Part II

CHAPTER 7 | **61**
Investing Principles

CHAPTER 8 | **69**
Doing Your Due Diligence

CHAPTER 9 | **81**
Execution! When to Buy & When to Sell

CHAPTER 10 | **89**
Crypto Currency

CHAPTER 11 | **101**
Taxes

CHAPTER 12 | **103**
Conclusion - The End

> Watch your thoughts,
> they become your words;
> watch your words,
> they become your actions;
> watch your actions,
> they become your habits;
> watch your habits, they
> become your character;
> watch your character,
> it becomes your destiny.

- LAO TZU -

CHAPTER 1

The Power of Your Thoughts

The thoughts you let inside your mind (through music, social media, TV, etc.) and the words you speak are two of the most powerful things that will EVER influence your life. Your thoughts and words will become your reality. Whatever you believe can happen, will happen.

If you strongly believe you can make a million dollars or become super successful then it can become your reality.

ON THE OTHER HAND, if you don't believe that you can accomplish your dreams and goals, *you're also probably right.*

The first step to getting the life you've been dreaming of is just **BELIEVING** that you can. Your belief will be the rocket fuel that pushes you to take action! Just like fuel, the right belief will boost you forward, but the wrong one will do more damage than good.

When I first heard this as a kid, I thought it was just something that people would say to try to inspire me to think more POSITIVELY.

So, I didn't pay attention to it. Looking back, I now realize how much our environment shapes our minds.

2 | NEW NERD MONEY

Peer pressure is a real thing. Group thinking is real too.

And as most kids do, we allow the thoughts of others to become our own thoughts. You start talking the same as the people around you. You start liking the same things that your friends like so you can fit in.

At times this can work for you, but it can also work against you.

The only reason I started playing basketball was because of my best friend. As a kid, he had the best Allen Iverson crossover that nobody could guard. He even believed that he could go to the NBA. His confidence was so contagious that he made me believe that I could do the same.

So I started playing ball. Even though I sucked at scoring, I was one of the best defenders in Chicago ("in my mind"). I ended up winning multiple AAU tournaments and did pretty decent in my short career.

The thing is, there are times when other people's thoughts and ideas can lower your confidence in yourself. When I was 5 years old I started taking Kung Fu (martial arts) and I loved competing. I believed I could do anything and I was fearless. It didn't hurt that I was actually pretty good at it too.

My thoughts allowed me to do things that most people couldn't dream of doing at my age. In just my first two years I won 1st Place in two tournaments and placed 2nd in another one. Being short as a kid, this was huge for me.

But once I stopped going to martial arts, I took on the mindset that my friends had from school. I became fearful, afraid of failing, afraid of making mistakes. I was even afraid of how other people thought of me.

Those negative thoughts held me back from reaching my full potential. I still got good grades in school, but I noticed that I was afraid of taking risks. Being afraid stopped me from getting better and going after more.

THE POWER OF YOUR WORDS

Your thoughts can lead to greatness or destruction. Whatever we constantly think about, we will begin to say out loud. I think you can agree, but we usually only say things that make sense to us or that we believe in. So, your words reflect how you feel and think.

A very wise and famous Chinese philosopher named Confucius once said, "He who says he can and he who says he can't are both usually right."

This might sound cheesy but your words really do have power. As crazy as that may seem, what you say can impact the world around you and even the relationships that you have with others.

MONEY MAYWEATHER

Floyd Mayweather Jr. is arguably the greatest boxer of all time. He's made hundreds of millions of dollars and is undefeated in his career with fifty wins and zero losses.

Coming out of fights with no cuts and bruises, he was given the nickname "Pretty Boy Floyd." But in 2012 he changed his nickname.

When he explained why he made the change, he said "When I changed it to Money Mayweather, I started Making Money. You gotta speak things into existence."

Since changing his nickname in 2012, he's earned over 600 million dollars in less than 15 fights. Now, this doesn't mean you will make millions just by saying it. No. Putting time and effort into your craft leads to results.

But by speaking what you want into reality, **you give yourself permission** to achieve your goals and dreams.

Our words can create or destroy. What you say can mean the difference between you achieving your dreams and goals or not achieving them. That's why we MUST pay attention to what we say and be careful of the words we allow to escape us.

You're probably wondering, "What in the world does this have to do with making money?"

The energy you put out into the world will always come back to you. If you say and believe that you can make money and be successful then it can happen. But, if you believe that you will never reach those goals then you won't.

We only go as far as we believe and not an inch further.

The book <u>The Twelve Universal Laws of Success</u> speaks on this.

> *"Your thoughts lead to feelings, your feelings lead to words, your words lead to actions and your actions create results."*

If you speak the world you want to create for yourself, then eventually you will take steps to make it happen.

AFFIRMATIONS

So is there anything we can do about changing our thoughts and controlling our words? YES there is.

The first thing we can do is change our self-talk through affirmations.

Affirmations are positive words we say to ourselves that boost our self-esteem.

This is one of the most powerful tools we can use to improve the way we feel about ourselves.

Again your words have power, so you have to speak the reality you want into existence.

Sometimes you gotta fake it till you make it. If you say it enough times eventually your affirmations can come true.

Here are a few affirmations that you can use.

And if you don't like these, that's ok, I won't get offended. Just create your own that work for you.

- I am strong
- I am wealthy
- I am in shape
- I am great
- I deserve to be happy
- I deserve to be successful
- Money comes to me easily and in abundance
- Opportunities come to me easily and in abundance
- Peace and Happiness come to me easily and in abundance

If you CONSISTENTLY read these affirmations out loud every day, it can make a huge difference over time. Sometimes we forget who we are and who we can become.

By saying these out loud, you remind yourself of who you are.

When you know who you are, you'll be encouraged to keep moving forward. I challenge you to read these affirmations 3 times a day, every single day!

If you can do that, you'll be able to bend reality to your will.

YOU ARE
enough

CONTROL YOUR INNER CIRCLE

Having the right people in your circle will lift you up and motivate you to keep going after your goals.

That's why it's important to have the RIGHT people around us. Your environment can be the difference between feeling insecure or confident. So be around those who want to see you win because they'll inspire you and give you confidence.

You might have friends who always talk bad about themselves. If they talk about what they can't do. If they make you feel like you can't be great, you should think about removing them. If you continue to spend time around this type of person, eventually you will have the same mindset as them.

Now, it might be difficult at times to change the people you're around. Some of them might be family which makes it almost impossible. The best way is to slowly stop talking to them.

Slowly stop responding to their texts, and interacting with them. If you do this, it will seem as though you just grew apart. But if you suddenly cut someone off, then their feelings may unnecessarily get hurt.

Once you can control your thoughts, your words, and your circle then eventually you will be able to control your reality. If you can control reality, there won't be anything you can't accomplish.

All you have to do is take that first step to make it happen.

So, let's step into our greatness BABYYYY!

Yesterday is history.
Tomorrow is a mystery.

Today is a gift that's why it's called the present.

Eleanor Roosevelt

> "You either master money, or, on some level, money masters you.

TONY ROBBINS

CHAPTER 2

It takes money to make money

WOW! You made it past personal development.

CONGRATULATIONS on making it to the financial literacy section.

Before we get into "building wealth" and "growing your money" we should first talk about making money.

The reality is, in most cases, it takes money to make money. It's very difficult to build wealth if we don't have money to begin with.

If you're a teenager or adult, it doesn't matter because the same rules apply. Even if you aren't worried about how to make money, it's still good to be aware of the different options.

There are three paths you can take.

The first path is working for someone by getting a job.

The second is the entrepreneur's route which is selling a product or service for a profit.

The third is investing. We will cover this one in a later chapter.

Let's start with the **entrepreneur's route**. This is my personal favorite!

So what is an "Entrepreneur"? They are **PROBLEM SOLVERS**.

That's it! They solve other people's problems and get paid well to do so. How much they make depends on how big the problem is and how good they are at fixing it.

A great example is Uber. Uber solved a problem by making it easier to travel without owning a car or taking a taxi. Now Uber makes billions of dollars every year. How about CashApp and Zelle? Both made it fast and easy to send money to other people and are billion-dollar companies.

Even Apple changed the way that we talk to each other and listen to music through iPhones. We can talk to anyone at any time and take our music with us everywhere. On June 30, 2023, Apple became the first company in the world to be worth $3 Trillion.

The people who created these companies are now Millionaires and Billionaires! But all of them started with the goal of creating solutions and making life easier for others.

By fixing problems, you not only make the world better but you can make TONS of money from it.

Make sure that you focus on solving problems. If your only goal is to make money, it will be very hard to find the success that you're looking for.

Isn't the whole point of this **to make money**? Yes, that is true. I used to think this way until I heard a quote.

> "If you want to make a million dollars, you have to solve a 10 million-dollar problem."

So if you can bring value to people, they will gladly pay you for it.

THE ENTREPRENEUR

Making money as an entrepreneur is not as hard as you think.

You can start by looking around you to see what people need.

All it takes is a little bit of creativity to make it happen.

Do some research on other ideas, then take it from there.

SOLVES A PROBLEM

Here's a list of different ideas to get you started:

- Babysitting
- Dog Walking and Pet Sitting
- Yard Work - mowing lawns, raking leaves, shoveling snow
- Freelance Work - writing, graphic design, or web development on Fiverr or Upwork
- Cutting Hair
- Retwist Hair
- Tutoring
- Washing Cars
- Tinting Car Windows
- Promoting Products as a Social Media Influencer
- Selling Candy

These are just some of the many ways you can make money through entrepreneurship.

Even if you don't like this list, there are thousands of other ways that you can get paid to help people around you solve their problems.

If you don't like the list, or see something that you can do, don't worry - these are just ideas and you probably have some amazing ones.

Once you pick your business idea, the next important step is figuring out how to make money from it.

Mr. Dame Dash, music mogul and Roca Fella Records Co-Founder, once said, "Know how you're gonna make money before you get into a business."

Many entrepreneurs (including myself) have suffered because they didn't know how to create income. To avoid this, you gotta know the game before you start to play it.

So before you start, make a list of at least 3-5 different ways your business can make money. If you can make a list of 5-10 then that's even better. This can be a list of things you can do today or in a few months.

If you're stuck, just Google: "How to make money in (*add your business*)?"

Here's an example of different ways a cameraman could earn income.
1. Record Weddings
2. Record Music Videos
3. Record Real Estate Walkthroughs
4. Edit videos (music videos, YouTube videos, documentaries, etc.)
5. Teach others how to edit videos
6. Rent equipment to others

If you can make a list of at least 5 different strategies, you're already ahead of most people.

But, if you struggle to come up with just 3, you should probably pick a different problem to solve.

Entrepreneurship: The Pros & Cons

There are many "pros" and many "cons" to starting a business. It can be the best thing to happen to you, but it can also be the worst if you're not ready.

This way of life is NOT for everyone!

Most entrepreneurs never reach success because getting their always takes longer than you think and costs more than anyone expects.

But if you stick with it, it can lead to some amazing results.

The Pros and Cons of Being an Entrepreneur:

PROS — Here are a few of the pros of becoming an Entrepreneur

- **Full Control of Work**: You get to be your own boss, choose your own projects, and make your own decisions.
- **Potential to Make a Lot of MONEY**: You have the potential to earn more money than you would at a job. By giving your customers what they need, you get to create as many products as you want and set the price of each one!
- **Creative Fulfillment:** Entrepreneurs can turn their ideas and passions into a business, making them feel fulfilled personally and creatively.
- **Flexible Schedule**: Having a flexible schedule allows you to decide when and how much you want to work.

> **CONS** — But with all the good things, come the bad. Here are some of the cons that come with being an entrepreneur.
>
> - **Responsible for Everything**: There's no one to hold you accountable. Without someone telling you what to do, it can be very easy to lose focus or procrastinate.
> - **Loneliness**: It can get very lonely, especially if you work from home or with a small team. This can lead to self-doubt or feeling overwhelmed with all the work and responsibilities.
> - **No Such Thing as Work-Life Balance**: You will need to spend most of your time, and attention on your business so it can grow. You may struggle to balance your work and personal life.
> - **Finding Customers and Making Money**: Finding customers is difficult, especially if you have competitors or you're just beginning. There will be times when you won't or will barely make enough to survive.

Being an entrepreneur isn't all sunshine and rainbows.

Before you get started ask yourself, "Is this something that I would be willing to do no matter what? Is my reason for becoming an entrepreneur big enough or important enough to hang in there when I'm not winning?"

MY STORY

When I was a kid, I was obsessed with making my OWN money.

I didn't want to depend on my parents or grandparents to get me what I wanted. But, I also was a problem solver. I hated having to go to school every day to eat that lunch. After I turned 8, it started to taste nasty and it just went downhill from there (no shade to school cafeterias).

The problem for me was that everyone in my family knew how to cook. My grandma was the best at cooking soul food. From fried shrimp to lamb chops and even sweet potato pie. My pops made the best burgers and steaks ever. And my mom was THE seafood expert, making salmon, shrimp alfredo, and even cookies (I'm getting hungry just writing this). I was used to having this amazing food all the time, and I couldn't stand eating bad food at school.

One day, I decided to start taking my mom's cookies to school so I wouldn't have to eat those rock-hard pears they served at lunch. When my friends saw them, they kept asking me if they could try some, so I let them. Once they got a taste, they couldn't get enough and they begged me for more.

Over the weeks, I asked my mom to keep making cookies. At the time, she didn't know I was secretly taking them to school and selling them to my friends. So when she found out, she couldn't believe what I was doing. I already made my money so there wasn't much she could do.

Eventually, I convinced her to keep making cookies by telling her how much the kids loved them and the benefits of selling them.

Fast forward to 7th grade, I became even more independent. Every day I would walk from school to Target and basketball practice. The problem was, I needed money so that I could eat after school before going to practice. I used to try to sneak in with the afterschool kids to grab food but they caught on. So, I had to come up with something else. My pops gave me the idea to start selling candy, and that's exactly what I did.

Every day before school, I would go to the gas station near my house and buy honey buns for 50 cents each. This was back when they were still cheap. I would take them back to school and sell them for $1. Every single day I was doubling my money. With the extra cash I made, I started selling Frooties.

Every week I would go to the candy store right off the I-94 Expressway and buy a bag of Frooties for $4.50. I took the entire bag and flipped it for $18. After 3 months of selling candy to only 30 kids in my grade, I made over $1k at 12 years old. So I used that money to buy my first phone.

All my friends had the same problem that I had. You've probably had this problem too. Not having good food to eat at school & and being hungry after school. All I did was sell them the solution. I didn't have to convince them to buy it and I didn't have to market it that much. That's why it was super easy to make money.

Moral of the story, **find a problem that a lot of people have then sell the solution**.

> Focus on doing amazing things in the world, and the money will come.
>
> — Jeff Hoffman

Working for Someone (a job): The Pros and Cons

Even though being an entrepreneur has its perks, again it's not for everyone.

Your other option is to work for someone / get a job. I know having a job may not be the best situation but think about it like this. You are getting PAID to LEARN!

Most of us who are teens, young adults, or even older don't have a lot of skills yet. But by getting a job, they will teach you those skills while also paying you.

We went to school for at least 13 years to learn for free, so why not get paid to do it instead?

Just like entrepreneurship, there are pros and cons to working for someone else. Here is a quick list of both.

PROS

- Steady income: Working a job gives you a steady source of income and you'll have peace of mind knowing you will get paid every week.
- Learning opportunities: A 9 to 5 job may have opportunities to learn new skills and gain experience in a specific field.
- Socialization: Working with colleagues allows you to be social and learn how to work with others.
- Work-life balance: Working a 9 to 5 job allows you to have a better work-life balance, due to having specific work hours.

CONS

- Limited independence: Having a job you'll have limited independence. With having a manager and a boss you must follow company rules and procedures.
- Limited flexibility: A 9 to 5 job typically has set hours, which means you can't schedule anything during those hours.
- Limited earning potential: Since you are paid at any hourly rate, you will only be able to make so much compared to having a business or being in a specialized career.
- Limited time for personal pursuits: The fixed hours of a 9 to 5 job means you won't have as much time for personal projects or pursuing business ideas.

WE DID IT. Pros and Cons done BABY!

Now you have a better understanding of why you should or why you shouldn't get a job.

You know I can't leave you hanging without giving you some ideas for different jobs. Here a list of different places or industries where you can find a job.

- **Grocery Stores** - Walmart, Trader Joe's, Mariano's, Kroger or Meijer have positions as cashiers, baggers, or stockers.
- **Clothing and Apparel Retailers** - H&M, Forever 21, Macy's, Lululemon, Footlocker, Zara, or any clothing store in the mall are all good options. Some of the jobs include helping customers, organizing merchandise, and keeping the store clean.
- **Fast Food Restaurants** - Some good places are McDonald's, Burger King, Chick-fil-A, Pizza Hut, Olive Garden, Wendy's or Taco Bell. Most are looking for crew members, cashiers, or food preparers.
- **Coffee Shops** - Starbucks, Dunkin' Donuts, or independent cafes, often hire for positions like baristas or cashiers.
- **Property Management Companies** - Looking to get into real estate? Property management companies can teach you how to manage homes without owning them.
- **Social Media Marketing** - Working at social media marketing companies you can learn how to create engaging content, manage and grow social media pages, and build marketing campaigns for products
- **Movie Theaters** - Some positions include ticket cashier, running concessions(food and drinks), cleaning crew, or usher at movie theaters.
- **Department Stores** - Popular Department stores like Target, or Nordstrom are great places to work. You can also work at home improvement stores like Home Depot, Lowes, or Ace Hardware are always good options.
- **Pet Stores** - PetSmart or local pet shops if you enjoy animals, involve helping customers with pet care products, feeding animals, and keeping the store clean.
- **Recreation Centers** - Local recreation centers or amusement parks like Six Flags are always looking for lifeguards, game attendants, cleaning crew, or concession workers(serving food and drinks).

These are just some of the many opportunities that could be available.

As you grow and find your passion there will be other careers that you can choose from Education, Tech, Engineering, Plumbing, Trucking, Production, to hundreds of others.

Once you choose your path, you will be able to earn even more money. When you get good enough, you could even get paid to teach others to do your job. That's where the real money comes in.

Unlike the last one, I don't have any stories of working at a job.

Many times, getting a job has been the first step that people take to reach financial success. If you decide to go this route, make sure your job is teaching you skills that will help you grow. If you want to be in social media, find a job that will teach you skills like content creation, and managing social media pages. Remember, find a place where you'll learn skills that you can put to use in your future career.

This chapter had a bunch of information, but it doesn't mean a thing if you don't get started. I don't care what you choose to do, go take that first step. If it's filling out that job application, or buying the supplies you need to start your entrepreneurship journey.

JUST DO IT! Get started today.

Don't wait for the perfect moment, because there will NEVER be a perfect moment. Whatever fears or worries you have, let them go.

All of the dreams you have for yourself and your family, that big house, that nice car, THE FREEDOM. The road to that life starts with you taking the first step and doing it!

just believe in yourself.

CHAPTER 3

Financial Literacy Basics

LADIES AND GENTLEMEN, IT'S TIME!

In this chapter, we're going to introduce some new words and ideas. You'll hear these terms a lot, so it's good to learn them. If you can understand what they mean, it will be much easier to grow in this space. This part should be easy because it's mostly about learning new words.

Everything that we buy falls into two categories: **Needs** or **Wants**. Either it's something we can't live without and need, or it's something that is a luxury which is a want.

Every time we buy something, we have to ask ourselves, "Is this something I need or something I want?"

Let me ask you this. Would you say that water and food are needs or wants?

Think about it for a second. Since we would die without both, they are indeed NEEDS. Now what about shoes? Let's take a pair of Jordan 1s for example, would you say they are a Need or a Want? In this case, they're just wants.

"But Ian, I need shoes to walk around in." If you were thinking this, you would be right about needing shoes. But do you really need to spend $200-$400 on a pair of shoes? You could buy a pair of Air Force 1s, vans, or even combat boots all less than $100. Knowing if something is a need or want helps us decide if we should purchase that item right now.

Income & Expenses

The very first financial terms my dad taught me at 6 years old, were **Income** and **Expenses**. As a 6-year-old, it was pretty easy to understand. Income is the money that you make or receive and an expense is the money you spend on something. Think of income as money going into your bank account and expenses as money leaving your bank account.

Let's say that you got paid from your job, that is income. Selling candy at school is definitely income too.

On the other hand, if you paid $10 for food, that's an expense. Or if you sent $15 to your friend for gas money, that's an expense.

Anything that would put money into your account is income, and anything that would take money out of your account is an expense.

Assets vs. Liabilities

Another pair of words that you'll hear a lot is **Assets** and **Liabilities**. Now there can be a whole debate on what an Asset is or what a Liability is. To keep this simple we're going to talk about this in terms of things that make or lose money.

WHAT'S WHAT?

Simply put, an **asset** is something that you own that has value, or can bring in more money.

For example, if you own a barbershop and you made $5,000 a month from it, the shop would be an asset.

Assets don't have to just be physical items. Your skills or knowledge can be assets too. Since you can use your brain and your skills to bring in money, that makes them assets.

On the other hand, **liabilities**, are things that don't add value and take money away from you. I know that some of you reading this book play video games. Let's take a PS5, as an example, that's a liability.

Before you freak out, there's a good explanation. The day you buy a new PS5, the value instantly drops. If you decide to resell it, you can never make money from it. On top of that, you have to pay for every additional game plus the in-game currency. You're constantly spending money with nothing coming back to you. Unless you're a pro gamer or a streamer who makes money, a PS5 isn't going to bring you income no matter how much you use it.

Therefore, it's a liability.

The asset and liability topic can get very confusing but it's all about how you use that item.

To make it easy, ask yourself this, "**Will I use this item to help me make money or at least help keep my money**?"

If the answer is Yes, then it's an Asset.

If the answer is No, then it's a Liability.

Financial Words to Know

savings — money you set aside for future needs or emergencies and it's usually kept in a bank account

budget — a plan that you create which helps you manage your income and expenses, setting limits on how much you can spend in different areas of your life

debt — when you owe someone or a company money, through a loan or a credit card. Borrowing money from the bank to buy a car would be an example of debt

interest — the cost of borrowing other people's money. Think of it as a fee for someone giving you their money

profit — the difference between how much you spend on something and how much you sold it for
Profit = Selling Price - Amount Spent

taxes — money that the government makes people, businesses or other entities pay to help keep our country going

inflation — when the prices of things we buy, like games, clothes, and food, keep going up over time. Inflation happens when the cost of making things, like clothes or food, goes up so businesses increase the prices of their products so they can still make money

return on investment — or ROI is a way to find how much money you'll make on an investment (using a percentage); the higher the ROI, the better
ROI = (Profit / Amount Spent) * 100

LET'S GOOOO!

We made it through all the terms and definitions.

Now look, you might need to read some of those words again and again, and that's fine.

It took me a while to understand most of these words and what they mean. It's an ongoing process of learning new information.

But once you are able to understand all of these concepts - you'll be UNSTOPPABLE!

To all you beautiful people, I'll see you in the next chapter.

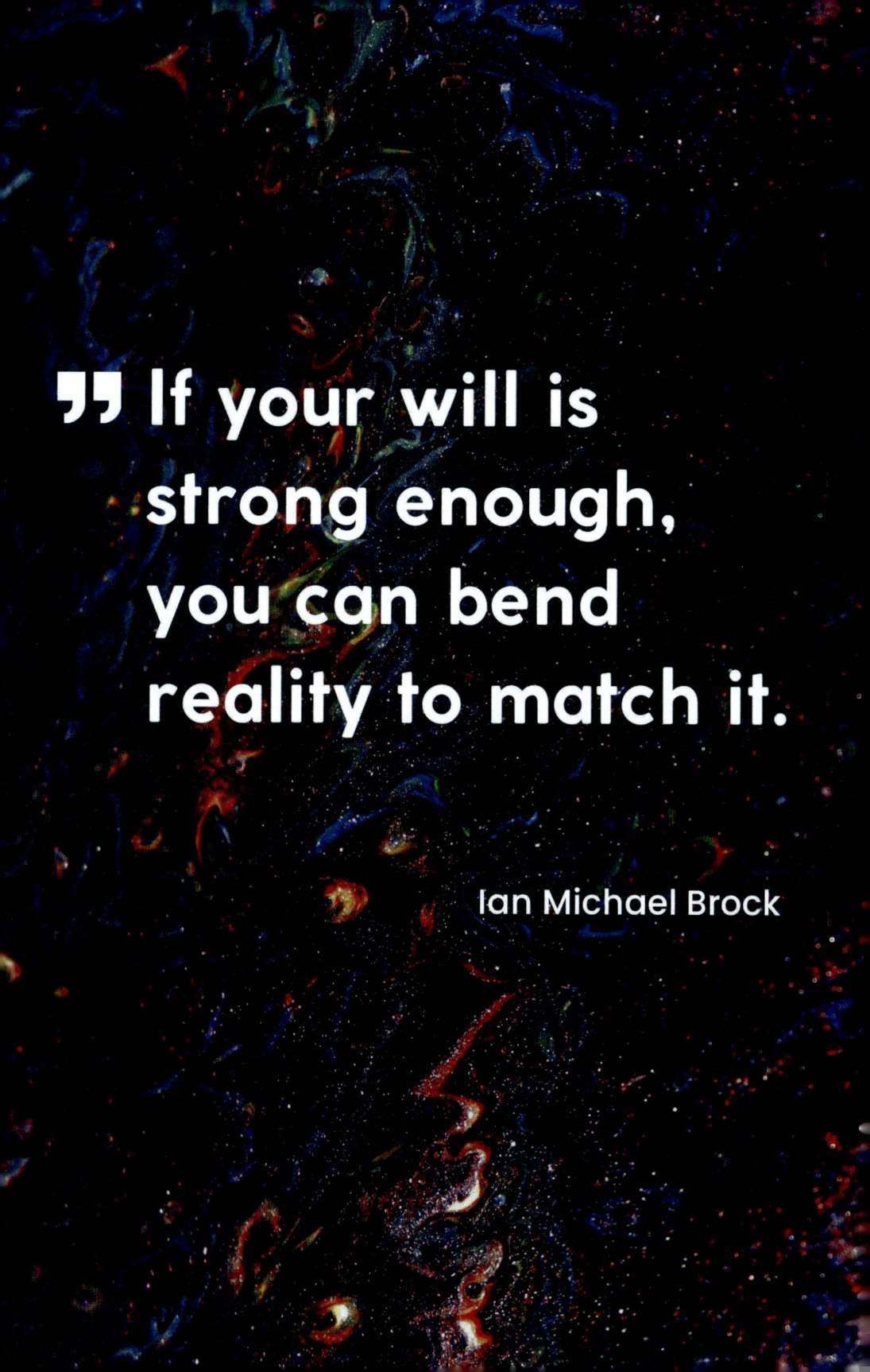

> You can make money two ways — make more, or spend less.

JOHN HOPE BRYANT

CHAPTER 4

Budgeting Your Money

BOOM! We've gone over basic terms and the different ways you can earn money.

Now that you've put some money in your pocket, it's time to make sure you keep it. The problem with money is, it's easier to make it than it is to keep it. As soon as we get money, there are bills to pay, we want to go shopping, TAXES, and so many other things that try to take our money away from us.

In this chapter, we're going to cover a tool that will help us manage and keep as much money as we can. That tool is a BUDGET!

So what is a budget? Think of it as a plan that helps you manage your money wisely. It's a way to keep track of how much money you have and where you spend it.

If we don't keep track of where our money goes, we tend to spend it recklessly. By keeping a budget, we can rest easy knowing where all of our money went instead of figuring out how it left us.

Going from making money to being broke because you don't know where you spent it is not a good feeling.

TRUST ME, I've been there before.

FINANCIAL CONTROL

By creating a budget, you become the boss of your money. You can decide how much you want to save for something special, like a new outfit or to go out with friends. You can even plan how much to spend on food, games, or hobbies you enjoy.

Budgeting is not about being strict with your money. It's about making sure you have enough for the things you need and the things that make you happy.

Goal Creation

So how do we create a budget?

The very first step is to make goals. At the end of the day, we're human and we have different emotions. If you're like me, then you probably forget a lot and have days when you don't feel like doing anything. That's why we need something to motivate us.

Goals give us that extra push we need and they remind us of why we're working so hard.

On top of that, writing down your goals increases the odds of you achieving them. Mr. Steve Harvey spoke on this in a YouTube video. He said that once you write down your goals, it is guaranteed that you will accomplish at least 10% of them. So we might as well write out exactly what we want.

creating
GOALS

One of the best methods to create goals is the **SMART Goals System**. This system is used to make it easier to create goals that you can track.

SMART is a secret code for Specific, Measurable, Achievable, Relevant, and Time-Bound

SPECIFIC — Be **specific** in the goals you want to accomplish.

MEASURABLE — Be able to **measure** and track the progress of your goals.

ACHIEVABLE — Your goals should challenge you, but still be **achievable**.

RELEVANT — Your goals should be **relevant** to what you want to get better at and what matters to you.

TIME-BOUND — Your goals need a deadline or a **time** to complete them. Having one helps you stay focused and gives you a sense of urgency.

IT'S YOUR TURN TO CREATE YOUR GOALS

It's time to use the SMART Goal System to create our own goals.

Grab a piece of paper and a pencil or open up the notes app on your phone so we can create our goals together.

CREATING GOALS

Starting with the T in SMART, we're going to set a deadline for when we want to accomplish all of our goals.

There are different types of goals you can create, for example:
- Yearly Goals
- Quarterly Goals
- Monthly Goals
- Weekly Goals

I find that quarterly goals are the most balanced. They give us just enough time to work on our goals but not too much time to procrastinate.

Since we're working on quarterly goals, **at the top** of your page write your deadline 3 months from today.

Think of what you want to accomplish in these next 3 months.

- How much money do you want to have saved up?
- Is there something expensive you want to buy like a phone or new shoes?
- Is there a place that you want to work at?
- Is there a business you want to start?

Write down all of the financial goals you want to accomplish over the next 3 months.

Make sure that these goals are as specific as possible and that you can track your results.

If you're having trouble, use the SMART goals system to help you.

Ask yourself if each goal is specific, measurable, achievable, relevant, and time-bound. Follow this system and you'll be good to go.

 **In case you're stuck on some of your goals, here are a few ideas to get you started**

EXAMPLE

Deadline August 31st

1. I will get a job at Target
2. I will save up $500
3. I will buy myself 3 new outfits
4. I will raise my credit score by 30 points
5. I will invest $750 into the stock market

BOOM! It's that simple! You just created your quarterly goals!

Congratulations, I'm proud of you.

But WAIT! There's still one more crucial step.

Now that you've created your goals, You **MUST READ THEM at least TWICE a day**. READ them when you first wake up and before you go to sleep at night.

Again, we get so busy that we forget a lot. Sometimes we just need a reminder. Reading our goals out loud is like using a map to show us which direction to go.

By speaking our goals into existence, we start working towards them. Which eventually leads to us accomplishing them.

Learning to Budget

Now that your goals are finished, it's time to create a budget. In any budget that you create, there should be 3 main categories: what you **Need**, what you **Want**, and your **Savings**.

NEEDS

Let's start with Needs. Our needs are things that we can't live without or NEED. Food, taking the bus to school/work, or bills like gas, and electricity are all needs. This should be the very first category that we put our money into since these things keep us alive and safe.

WANTS

The second category that we should put our money into is our wants. Wants are things that we want but can live without. Getting your hair and nails done, buying a new video game, and buying $400 shoes, are all examples of wants. They make our lives better but we don't need them.

SAVINGS

The last area is our savings. For savings, it all depends on what your goals are. Do you want to save up money for a new phone? BOOM, put it in your savings.

Do you want to eventually invest in stocks or real estate? Put money into your savings to use in the future. If you want to put money away for emergencies, put it in your savings.

Having savings can help you reach your goals faster but it can also save you.

Let's face it, stuff goes wrong all the time. Sometimes we need extra funds to help us out. So setting money aside in case of an emergency can save you from many situations.

LET'S GO! Now that you understand the basics, let's go to the next step.

The thing is, there are MILLIONS of different ways you can budget. So we're going to keep it simple.

50-30-20 RULE

One of the most popular strategies for budgeting is the **50-30-20 rule**.

This rule says that **50%** of your money should go to your **NEEDS**, **30%** of your money goes to your **WANTS**, and **20%** of your money goes into your **SAVINGS**.

Imagine you worked at the mall and made $1,000 in a week.

If we use the 50-30-20 rule, here's what it would look like:

50-30-20 Rule with $1,000

50% goes into **Needs** = $500
30% goes into **Wants** = $300
20% goes into **Savings** = $200

WHOOP WHOOP. You just learned how to create a budget. You see how simple that was!

So every time you earn money, use the 50-30-20 rule to keep you organized.

Again, I'm so proud of you for making it this far into the book.

Keep going, you're so much closer to achieving the success you've always wanted.

TRIAL & ERROR

It's important that your budget helps you get closer to your goals.

If your goal is to save $500 in 3 months but your budget won't get you there in time, make changes that you feel will work for you. Instead of 20% going into your savings maybe change it to 25%.

All of this is about trial and error. It's ok if you don't get it right the first time. It might take a few tries before you figure it out.

Don't get discouraged. If you find that this method doesn't work, adjust the numbers and try something different until it works for you.

DELAYED GRATIFICATION

These are all great lessons but it doesn't mean a thing if we don't follow them.

One of the biggest challenges I had was not spending my money as soon as I got it.

It's so tempting to go out and treat yourself.

You worked so hard for your money so why not get a reward?

But sometimes, you have to delay buying the things you want now, so you can have the future you want later. Trust me, you will struggle with this which is normal. I did, so you're not alone!

When it happens, remind yourself of your goals and the future you want.

I'm not the type to do something if I don't see the value in it. So if you can understand why you're making the sacrifice, it'll be easier to follow your plan.

This is easier said than done. But if you can stay disciplined and stay focused, then you can have everything you want in life.

CHAPTER 5

Understanding Credit - Part I

Have you ever wondered how so many people are living the dream life?

How do people always have the nicest clothes, and the nicest cars, and go on exotic vacations?

Ever since I was 13, I've been trying to find answers to those questions.

For the longest time, I couldn't understand how everyone looked rich.

Then I finally found the answer. This whole time a lot of it had to do with credit. Credit was the key that many people used to unlock the door to their dream lifestyle. Social media makes it seem like everyone is living that dream life.

Online everyone has Hellcats, BMWs, Lambos, Benzs, and big houses. But most of them don't buy with cash. They borrow money from a bank to get what they want.

When I found this out at 15, my pops and I created a plan to get my credit right.

As soon as I turned 18, we put the plan to work. In just the first 15 months of my credit journey, I built a 760 FICO score (credit score) and I had access to $20,000 in credit.

The average FICO score (credit score) for most adult Americans is 716. I'm bringing this up because your age doesn't have to stop you from getting access to what you want.

With the right knowledge, discipline, and execution you will be able to get this credit thing going.

In this chapter, I'm going to share the information that changed my life forever.

I hope you're ready. Grab your notebooks and snacks. You're in for a treat.

What is Credit?

Like many of us, you probably didn't have rich parents who could give you a million dollars. Even if you were lucky to have parents who could give you a lot of money, having those funds without the right education could be dangerous. If you don't know how to manage and grow your money, you'll end up losing it.

Having skills that help pay the bills is a must, but even that isn't enough.

Back in the day, people had to get creative. To get to the next level, they learned how to use other people's money to become rich.

THE ORIGINS OF CREDIT

Credit is a very powerful tool because it lets you buy things that would be hard to get if you don't have enough money. Like all good things, if used wrong, credit can hurt you if you abuse it to buy unnecessary stuff.

Originally, credit was created so we could borrow other people's money and use those funds to create ways to make more money.

In the 1600s, Voyagers needed money and resources to explore new land. So they went to wealthy people to get loans. This was called business credit. Those loans allowed them to make money so they could explore new territories without having to spend their own cash. Now, credit has opened the door to new ways to create wealth.

Imagine you had access to $50,000 in credit to start your new business. What if you had access to $400,000 in credit to buy that house you want? How much of a difference would that make? Having credit makes it easier to do what we want without having millions.

Again I'm not a financial advisor so you must DO YOUR OWN RESEARCH! With that being said, let's dig deeper into it!

TYPES OF CREDIT

So, what exactly is credit?

Credit is when you borrow money to buy something you want right now, but you promise to pay it back later when you have the money. On top of paying it back, there's usually an extra fee added called **interest**.

There are different ways you can borrow money or use "credit." Here are just a few examples:

> ★ Credit Cards
> ★ Department Store/Retail Credit Cards
> ★ Mortgages - (Loans to buy a house)
> ★ Car Loan or Auto Loan
> ★ Student Loans - (Loans to pay for college)
> ★ Personal Loans

WHAT IS A CREDIT SCORE?

To get approved for any type of credit, banks need to know if you are trustworthy and if you'll pay them back.

One of the ways they do this is to look at your "credit score". Think of your credit score like a report card that tells banks, credit unions, or lenders how good you are at paying back money that you borrow.

You can also think of it like a rating in 2K or a level on a battle pass in Fortnite or Warzone. The higher your rating or level is, the more you can do with your player. It's the same thing with your credit score.

CREDIT SCORE & CREDIT PROFILE

BELOW 600
NOT GREAT

600-680
FAIR

680-740
GOOD

740-790
GREAT

800+
EXCELLENT

When people give you money, they are taking a risk because they don't know if you will pay it back. That's why they check your credit score, to see how good you are with handling money. This helps them decide if it's safe to lend to you.

The higher your score, the better your chances are of getting approved for credit since it shows that you are responsible with money.

There are many different types of credit scores. The most widely used is called a "FICO Score" and it ranges between 300 to 850 points.

HERE'S WHAT YOUR SCORE MEANS

Your **goal** is to have **a 760+ credit score.** With a 760+ FICO score (credit score) you get the best deals and pay lower interest rates (fees) at this range

The Credit Score Formula

Your credit score is based on a formula that is determine by these 5 categories

1. Payment History (35%)
2. Credit Usage (30%)
3. Length of Credit (15%)
4. Mix of Credit (10%)
5. Amount of New Credit / number of Inquiries (10%)

#1 PAYMENT HISTORY - 35%

This is the **most important factor of your score** and it's pretty simple.

All you have to do is **PAY YOUR BILLS ON TIME**! Having a perfect payment history is key to having a high score. If you miss even one payment, your score can drop up to 150 points in some cases.

#2 CREDIT USAGE - 30%

Your Credit Usage is the second highest factor of your credit score. This is how much of your credit card you use each month. Let's say you have a credit card with a limit of $100. If you spend $30 on that card, your credit usage is 30%.

To get the best results and increase your score the most, YOU MUST keep your usage under 10%. So if you have a credit card with a limit of $1,000, what's 10% of that my people?

You guessed it - that would be $100. Remember the lower your usage, the better.

#3 LENGTH OF CREDIT - 15%

This one is pretty easy. The longer you've been using credit and paying it back, the higher your credit score will be.

It's like cooking on Thanksgiving. Everyone trusts grandma to make Thanksgiving dinner. Why? Because she's been doing it for years. But no one trusts that one cousin to cook because they have no experience and might burn the kitchen.

The same applies here. By having a longer history it shows that you are experienced with managing money. You can't do anything to control this but wait, make your payments on time, and be patient. Well, there is something you can do to speed up this process but that's a story for another book.

#4 MIX OF CREDIT - 10%

As we know, credit comes in different forms. There are credit cards, mortgages, car loans, and others.

By having different types of credit, it shows lenders that you can handle different responsibilities.

#5 AMOUNT OF CREDIT - 10%

The last part of the formula is the amount of new credit that you have. Every time you get approved for a new loan or a credit card in the last two years you will get a hard inquiry or a soft inquiry.

A hard inquiry lets lenders know that you've been looking for new credit, showing that you owe more people money. When you owe a lot of people, that's not a good look. This shows up on your credit report for lenders to see.

And If you have too many, you'll be denied!

Then there are soft inquiries. Soft inquiries aren't reported, so lenders can't see them when they look at your credit. This is a good thing for you.

Imagine somebody asking you if they could borrow $100 when you know they owe five other people the same amount. Would you be willing to lend them your money? Probably not because you don't know when or if you'll get your money back.

Having a lot of hard inquiries could drop your score. To avoid this, space out your applications for new credit. Your goal should be to have less than three hard inquiries in the last two years.

LET'S TEST WHAT WE LEARNED

If you were to give someone a loan for $15,000, which of these 2 people would you lend your money to?

Person A
- 1 Credit Card with a limit of $2k
- Never missed a payment
- Keeps utilization under 10%

Person B
- 3 Credit Cards with limits of $5k, $7k, and $15k
- 1 Car Loan of $12k and paid off
- Never missed a payment
- Keeps utilization under 10%

Out of these two, you would probably pick Person B.

Why? They not only have higher limits, but they have 3 credit cards and a paid-off car loan. Person B's history shows that they can be responsible with multiple types of credit.

That's why it's important to have a good mix of credit. It makes you look good to the bank.

> The desire of gold is not for gold.
>
> It is for the means of freedom and benefit.

Ralph Waldo Emerson

CHAPTER 6

Understanding Credit - Part II

Boom! Now you know all the things that make up your credit score.

Great job, I'm proud of you.

But that's just the first part. The next important step is to understand your credit profile (also known as your credit report). There is a HUGE difference between your credit score and your credit report.

Your credit score just shows how risky you are to the banks.

On the other hand, your credit report shows your history of borrowing money and paying it back. It has information about any loans or credit cards that you have. It also shows if you pay your bills on time, and if you owe anyone money.

Think of your Credit Score as a grade, and your credit report as your school transcript.

So how exactly do we get a good credit profile?

Here are five ways to help you build a strong profile:

1. NEVER MISS A PAYMENT
2. Keep your utilization under 10% with every credit card you have
3. Have a good mix of credit. Aim to have three credit cards and two loans (this will take time to get!)
4. Have less than three inquiries across the three credit bureaus
5. Have a 2+ year average length of credit (the time you've had credit for)

CREDIT BUREAUS

You might be wondering, "What in the world is a credit bureau?"

A credit bureau is a company that makes money by keeping track of your credit history. Their job is to collect information on your loans, credit cards, and how well you pay your bills. With this data, they create your credit report and your credit score.

There are three main credit bureaus: Experian, Equifax, and Transunion. These three bureaus don't talk to each other AT ALL. They're like those Aunties in the family that hate each other. They'll talk about each other, but not to each other.

Since each bureau operates differently, you will get 3 different credit scores and credit reports, instead of getting just one. There might be times when your credit score is 760 with Experian. But you'll have a 720 with Equifax and a 700 with Transunion.

I know this might seem weird but, each one is a separate company and they just move differently.

WHOOP WHOOOP! YOU ARE AMAZING!
YOU ARE BASICALLY A PRO AT CREDIT

How to get started

FINALLY! You've learned about credit and how to build your credit score.

You even learned how to set up a solid credit profile.

So how do we get started?

Here is a step-by-step plan to help you start building your credit:

1. Open a checking and savings account at a bank or credit union
2. Make deposits into your bank account
3. Save $250+ and use that money to open a secured credit card
4. FOLLOW THE RULES FOR SUCCESS - Pay your bills on time and keep your Utilization at 10% or lower

STEP #1 - OPENING YOUR BANK ACCOUNT

If you haven't already, you must open a checking and savings account at a bank or a credit union. Choosing the right place to put your money is super important. The bank you decide to go with is the same bank you will later open your credit card with.

Here are some things that you should look out for when choosing a bank:

- Are there monthly fees for having an account?
- Do they offer a secured credit card? (important for step #3)
- Do their credit cards have good rewards or low interest rates?
- How much money will you make each year from your account? (some offer 0.01%, while others offer up to 4%)

I would suggest that you start with a credit union.

Credit Unions are non-profits, so they aren't looking to take advantage of customers to make money. They often have better rates and have pretty good products. I personally bank at Navy Federal which is the best Credit Union out there. Some Other Credit Unions to pick from are PenFed and DCU.

If you choose not to go with a credit union, you can always go with a bank. When you're selecting a bank, make sure to research what their credit card products look like. This will be important because you may want to get more cards from them in the future. Some good banks to start with are Discover or Bank of America.

STEP #2 MAKE DEPOSITS INTO YOUR ACCOUNT

Now that you've opened up your bank account, it's time to deposit some money.

Every time you earn income, deposit it into your bank account. Your goal is to build a good relationship with your bank. When you put money into your account, you make them happy by giving them what they want.

When the bank is happy, they'll be more than willing to give you what you want and help you. It's like getting on your mom's good side so she's more likely to say yes when you ask for something.

STEP #3 OPEN A SECURED CREDIT CARD

Now it's time to get that secured credit card.

A secured credit card is a special type of card that helps you build credit. To get this card you need to put down a deposit. In case you can't pay your bill, the bank will just take the money from your deposit to pay off the card. It's actually a smart move because it's like having a backup plan.

To get started, you need to save at least $250 (the more the better). Once you've saved up your deposit money, you can apply for your card. Don't forget, you have to be at least 18 years old to do this step.

Some credit unions will upgrade you to an unsecured credit card after just 6 months of making on-time payments. They'll even give you back your deposit money. But with other banks, it could take 12 months for them to upgrade you, if they upgrade you at all. Unfortunately, every bank and credit union is different.

That's why it's important to do research before choosing a bank.

STEP #4 FOLLOW THE RULES FOR SUCCESS

Last but not least, make sure that you follow BOTH of these rules.

These rules are SUPER IMPORTANT if you want to build your credit faster.

Rule #1: Make your payments on time
Rule #2: Keep your credit usage under 10%

That's it! If you follow these two rules each month, you will be GOLDEN!

YOU DID IT

You finally made it through all of that information.

Give yourself a pat on the back.

You should be proud of yourself for making it this far. When you apply this information the right way, it can be worth millions of dollars in the future.

I'm so proud of you. This was definitely a tuff chapter. You're doing an awesome job, go ahead and take a break, then let's move on to the next one.

JUST KEEP GOING.

AN INVESTMENT IN KNOWLEDGE PAYS THE BEST INTEREST

— BENJAMIN FRANKLIN —

CHAPTER 7

Investing Principles

There's a saying that goes, "**How you do one thing is how you do everything**." The same applies to investing.

Some of the principles that you use when investing in stocks, can be used in other investments like real estate, business or even crypto. So now it's time to learn some of these principles that you can use to grow your money even more.

Why Investing is Important

The only true way to become wealthy is by making money in your sleep. This is the ultimate freedom. It takes time to get to this point and it doesn't happen overnight. But compared to the other options it's the best choice.

Imagine making 1% per year off of $100.

That's only $1 every year, which is terrible. That's what happens when you leave ALL of your money in a savings account.

But what if there was a way for you to make up to 50% on your money in your sleep?

What if I told you that with just the basic principles you could reach success and have your money work for YOU? Well, you're in luck because one of the ways to get this done is through stocks.

> **DISCLAIMER**: HIGHER RETURNS ON YOUR MONEY, LIKE THE ONE MENTIONED, ARE HIGH RISK INVESTMENTS. THIS MEANS THAT YOU HAVE A HIGHER CHANCE OF LOSING ALL OF YOUR MONEY.
>
> THE HIGHER THE RETURN (OR THE MORE YOU MAKE) ON YOUR MONEY THE HIGHER THE RISK. THE LOWER THE RETURN ON YOUR MONEY, THE LOWER THE RISK.

What Are Stocks?

So what are stocks?

Stocks are pieces of a company that you can purchase. Buying a stock makes you a part owner of that company. If the company grows and makes more money, the piece you own goes up in value and you can sell it for a profit.

You can become an owner of some of the biggest companies in the world. Apple, Microsoft (Xbox), Nike, Walmart, and Starbucks are just some of the ones you can invest in. When you are an owner of these companies, they work for you and make you more money.

There are many different ways to invest in stocks.

Here are the top three ways to get it done:

1. **Day Trading**,
2. **Swing Trading**, and
3. **Long-term Investing**

Day Trading is when you buy and sell a stock within the same day.

Swing Trading is when you buy and sell a stock within 1 year.

Long-Term Investing is when you buy a stock and hold it for at least a year before you sell it.

We are going to focus on long-term investing only.

Ok my beautiful people, buckle up because it's about to be a fast ride. Follow me on this journey to better understand **"The Game Of Stocks."**

Long-term investing is one of the better options. Once you put your money in the market, All you have to do is let your money grow over time. You don't have to read charts or look at the news, you can just forget about it. Of course, after you've found a good company to invest in.

If you know anything about Uncle Sam (the Government/the IRS), you know he's always looking for his money.

Luckily, the taxes you pay on long- term investing are way lower than the other two strategies (by at least 10%).

So Save Money, Live Better, and Invest Long Term!

TERMS & DEFINITIONS

Before we get into the basics, there are a few words that you should know. Here's a list of beginner stock terms and definitions:

01 Stock/Share
A stock is a small piece of a company that you buy. When you purchase stock you own a little part of that company.

02 Stock Market
The stock market is like a big marketplace where you can buy or sell pieces of different companies.

03 Stock Portfolio
A portfolio is a collection of stocks that a person owns. Think of this as your roster of different players. Instead of players, it's the different stocks you own.

04 Bull Market
A bull market is a period when most stock prices in the market are going up. When Bull Markets happen, people believe that the economy is going well. This leads to people feeling good about investing in companies.

05 Bear Market
A bear market is a period when stock prices overall are going down. This usually means things are not going well in the economy. So people don't feel good about investing in companies.

06 All-Time High
The All-Time High or ATH Is the highest price a stock has reached since it was first created.

07 Industry
A group of companies that sell similar business products or services.

Now that you understand a few basic terms, you are ready to go!!!

FINDING THE BEST COMPANY

One of the hardest decisions when investing in stocks is figuring out which company is the right one for you. Unlike what some might think, It's actually not that complicated. It's very similar to figuring out who the best NBA players are or the best rappers.

So we're going to keep this as simple as possible.

There are about 5 questions that you need to ask when choosing the right company.

If you can answer all of those questions with a yes then you should be in a good position to win. I'm not guaranteeing you will succeed 100% of the time, but your odds will definitely increase.

Here are the 5 questions:

1. Is it easy to understand how the company makes money?
2. Is this company in the top 3-5 of its industry?
3. Does this company have the potential to grow?
4. Does the company's stock chart go up and to the right? (If not, don't invest in it)
5. Is the All-Time High within the last 5 years? (If not, don't invest in it)

Just like that, you learned one of the hardest parts of investing.

Now that you finished Level 1, let's dive deeper and move on to Level 2.

> Huge shoutout to **Ian Dunlap** the "Master Investor," and **Wall Street Trapper** for sharing much of the information found in this book.
>
> I learned a ton about stocks from them on YouTube.
> It's a must to give credit where credit is due.

> Life is like riding a bicycle.
>
> To keep your balance, you must keep moving.

— Albert Einstein

STOP DREAMING
START DOING

CHAPTER 8

Doing Your Due Diligence

Throughout this book, I've mentioned the word RESEARCH multiple times.

But what does this word even mean?

Wernher Von Braun once said, "**Research is what I'm doing when I don't know what I'm doing.**"

So let's get informed so we know exactly what we're doing.

With stocks, there are two types of research you can do: Fundamental Analysis and Technical Analysis.

FUNDAMENTAL ANALYSIS

Fundamental Analysis is a way to find a company's real value. This is the research you do without looking at a stock chart. You can look for what the company sells and how much they make. You can even check to see if they have an advantage over other companies similar to them in the industry.

TECHNICAL ANALYSIS

Technical Analysis is a little different. It involves looking at a stock chart to see the price history. The goal is to try and predict where the price will go in the future.

Let's be real, no one wants to look at a bunch of spreadsheets to figure out if a company is good or not. To keep things simple, we're going to start by searching for a few things.

The very first thing you should look up is **how the company makes money** and **if the company is profitable**.

Let's take a look at Apple for example.

They make money by selling tech products and services. Products like iPhones, MacBooks, AirPods, and Apple Music. Now we know how they make money.

In the second quarter of 2023, they made $19.88 BILLION in profit. I don't know about you, but that sounds like a lot of profit to me.

We now have the answers to both questions. If it's hard to figure out what a company sells, then something fishy may be going on. To avoid this, we only want to pick companies that have real products and services. With Apple, you can find what they sell and how much they make on Google.

Doing this research is important because you need to know where you are putting your hard earned money. It's like picking a star player for your team.

We need to look at their stats and watch their game tape to make sure they can get buckets. The same thing goes for stocks. If you need help finding this info, Google it or use StockAnalysis.com.

Invest in the Top 3

I don't know about you, but I like buying clothes.

When I'm looking for a fit, I'm always looking for the best quality that's within my budget. If the quality is bad, then I know it's not going to last long. I use this same mindset when it comes to stocks.

When looking for the right company, we only want to go for the best.

Investing in a company at the bottom is risky since they haven't shown us they can make money.

To find the quality ones, all we have to do is stay in the top 3-5 of each industry. If they're at the top, that means they're reliable and can get the job done.

If you had to bet money on LeBron James winning or the guy at the end of the bench, who would you bet on? I hope you'd pick LeBron. He's one of the best to play the game and he's proven it multiple times.

So when it comes to investing in stocks, invest in those who've proven their worth.

Finding out if they're the best, isn't as hard as you think. Start by looking up the industry that the company is in (or use stock analysis to find out).

After that, Google the top 5 companies in that industry. If the company you've chosen is consistently in the top 5, then you've got yourself a good one! If not, it's time to find another pick for your roster.

A great example is Apple. Apple is in the Consumer Electronics Industry. We know they're one of the best because they are the first company to have a market value of $3 Trillion. If that doesn't say they're in the top 5, I don't know what will.

Again, we want to put ourselves in the best position to succeed. So why risk investing in a company that hasn't proven itself?

DOES THE COMPANY HAVE THE POTENTIAL TO GROW?

We know how our company makes money and that they're in the top 5 of their industry. The last part is to figure out if it has room to grow. The company might be one of the best now, but that doesn't mean they will stay there forever.

If your company doesn't innovate and create new products that people want to buy, they won't continue to make money. If they stop profiting, then we owners (or investors like YOU) start losing money.

To make sure that's not the case, find out what products the company plans to release.

Do they plan to expand into other industries? Is there a big market for the products that they plan to sell? Doing this research to see if this company has a bright future, will save you a bunch of money down the line.

Understanding How to Read Charts

Now that we've covered some of the fundamental analysis, it's time to move on to technical analysis.

This one is pretty easy. We're going to learn how to read a stock chart. Simple!

There are a few free websites that you can use to look at charts.

The easy one is **StockAnalysis.com** which is a fan favorite.

A more detailed one that I like to use is **TradingView.com**.

Even **CashApp** has stock charts that you can look at.

Like we learned in school about charts, a stock chart has two axes.

The horizontal line (the one at the bottom) is the x-axis and shows how much time has passed. This could be over the past few days, weeks, months, or years.

The vertical line (the one going up and down) is the y-axis. This represents the price of the stock. The more you move up, the higher the price gets. The more you move down, the lower the price is.

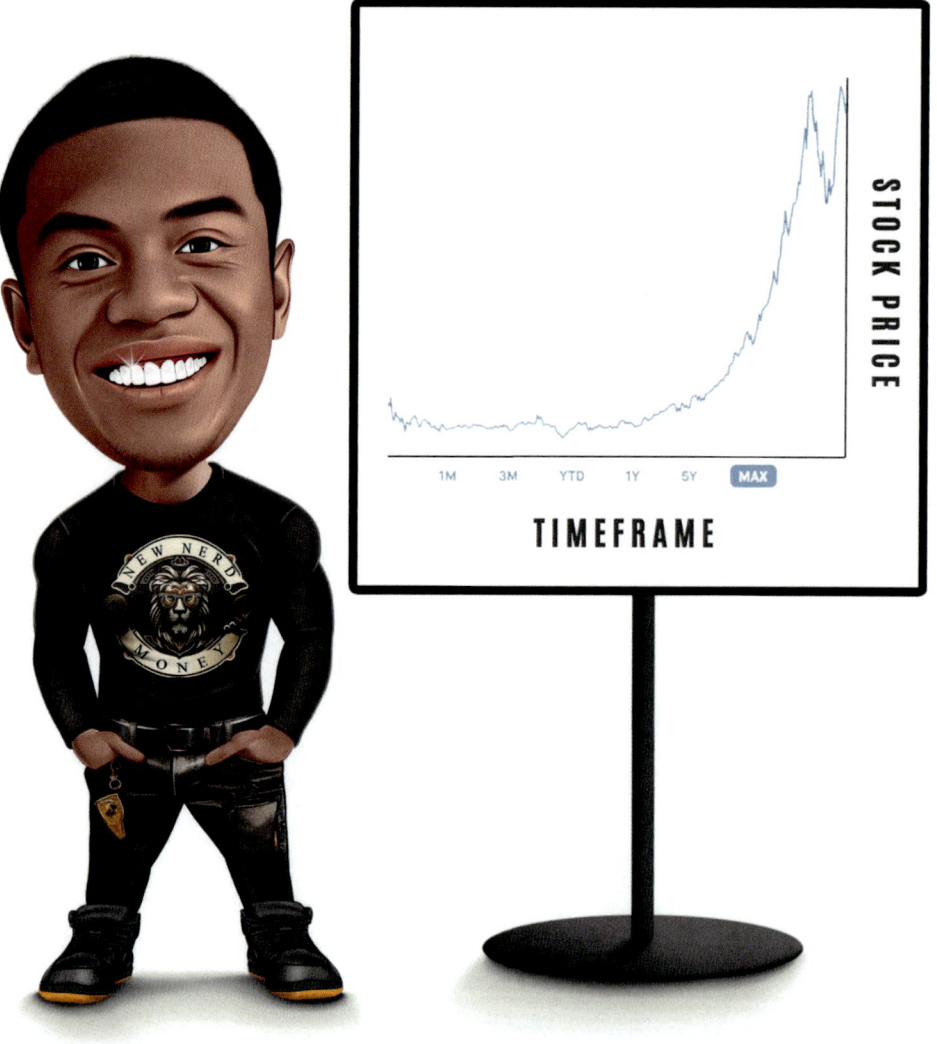

Look at that, you just learned how to read a stock chart. See how simple that was?

The next part of the chart is the time frames.

Stock charts can show the history of stock prices, within the last week, month, year, or even 5 years.

Each time frame gives you a different view of how the price moved.

Shorter ones are typically used for day trading.

But since we are focused on long-term investing, we will be using the longer ones.

TECHNICAL ANALYSIS

So let's pull up those stock charts. Between CashApp, StockAnalysis, or TradingView, pick the one that works for you.

To look up a company, you have to type its ticker symbol. A ticker is a shortened version of a company's name. Think of it as a code name or a nickname. For example, Apple's ticker is AAPL.

Once you find the ticker and pull up the chart, look for the MAX time frame and click it. This is going to show you the chart from the first day this company went on the market to the present.

The main thing we're looking for is consistency.

Does the line on the graph go up and to the right? If it does, that means the company is a good pick. Since the price of the stock has consistently grown, it will more than likely continue to grow.

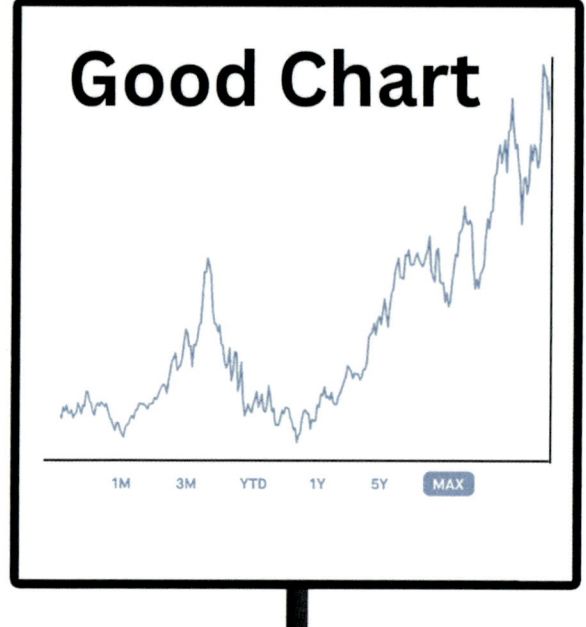

But if the company's chart is going down and to the right, this company is garbage.

Imagine you were working at a job and they paid you less and less every paycheck.

That would have me heated and I'd just leave. So you should be furious too and leave that company alone.

FINDING THE ALL-TIME HIGH

GREAT! We have a company that has a nice-looking stock chart.

Now it's time to find the company's all-time high.

Remember, the all-time high is the highest stock price a company has ever reached. To find the all-time high, select the max time frame. Your chart should look like this.

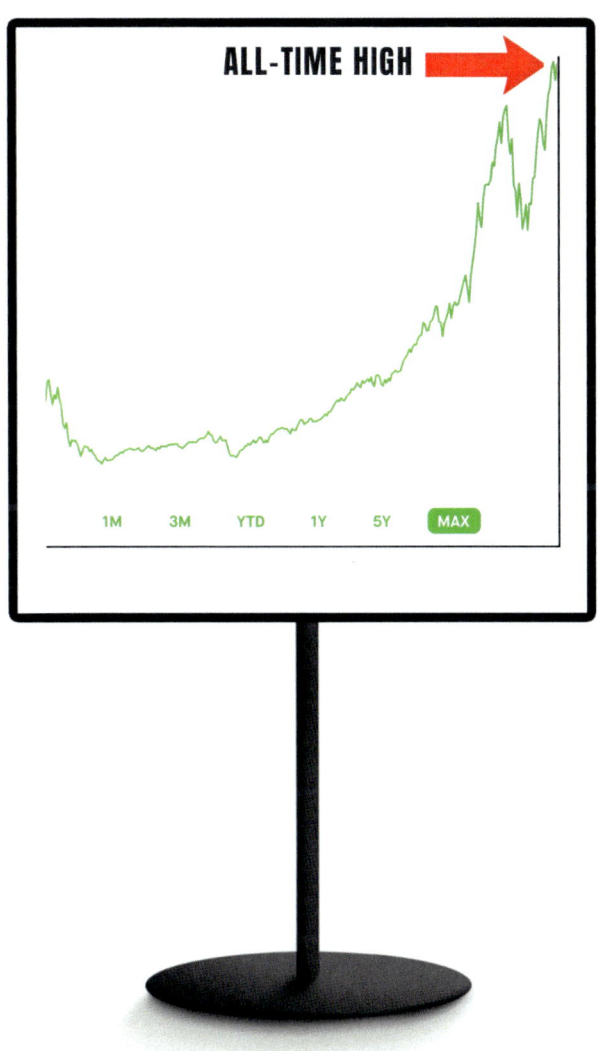

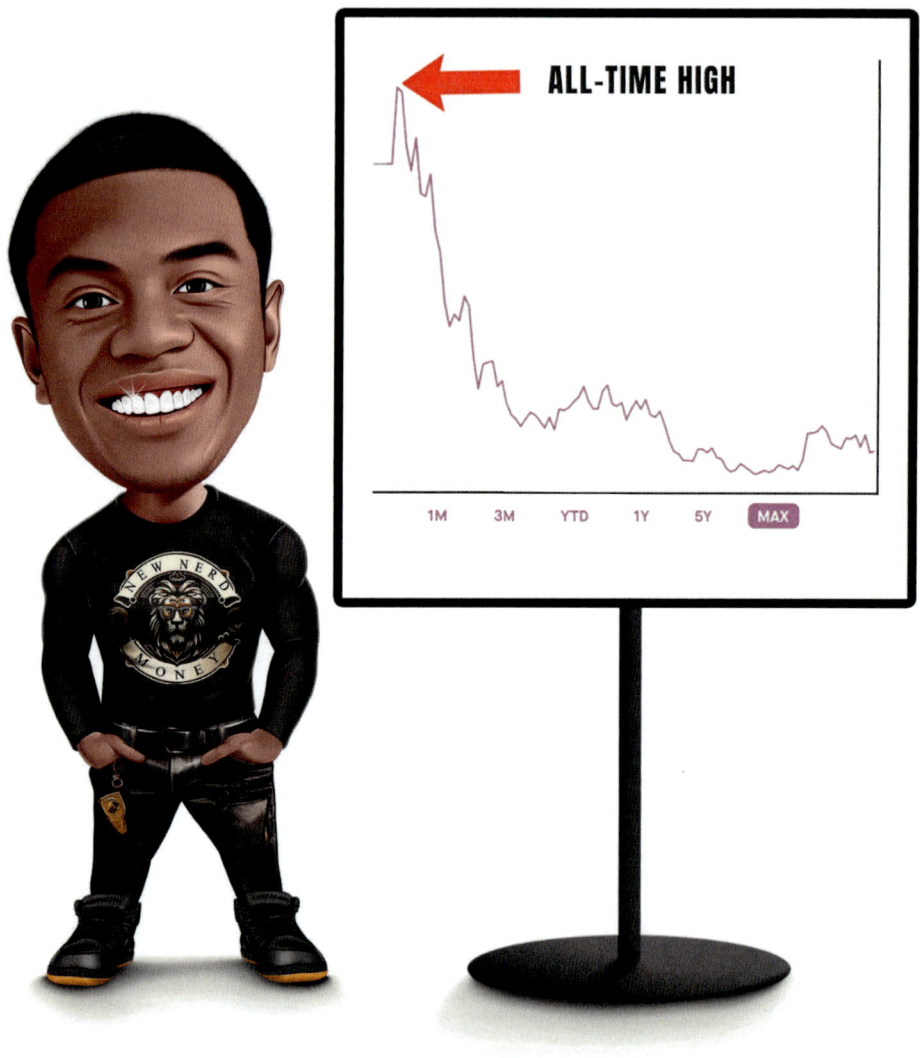

If the highest point of the line isn't within the last 5 years, you should probably leave that company alone.

This means the company peaked more than 5 years ago and hasn't been the same.

If it's been that long since they've been at their best, chances are they won't make a comeback.

BOOM!

You now know how to find good companies to invest in!

If you continue to practice and combine the Fundamentals with the Charts, you will become a company finding SNIPER!

When you do common things in an uncommon way, you will command the attention of the world.

George Washington Carver

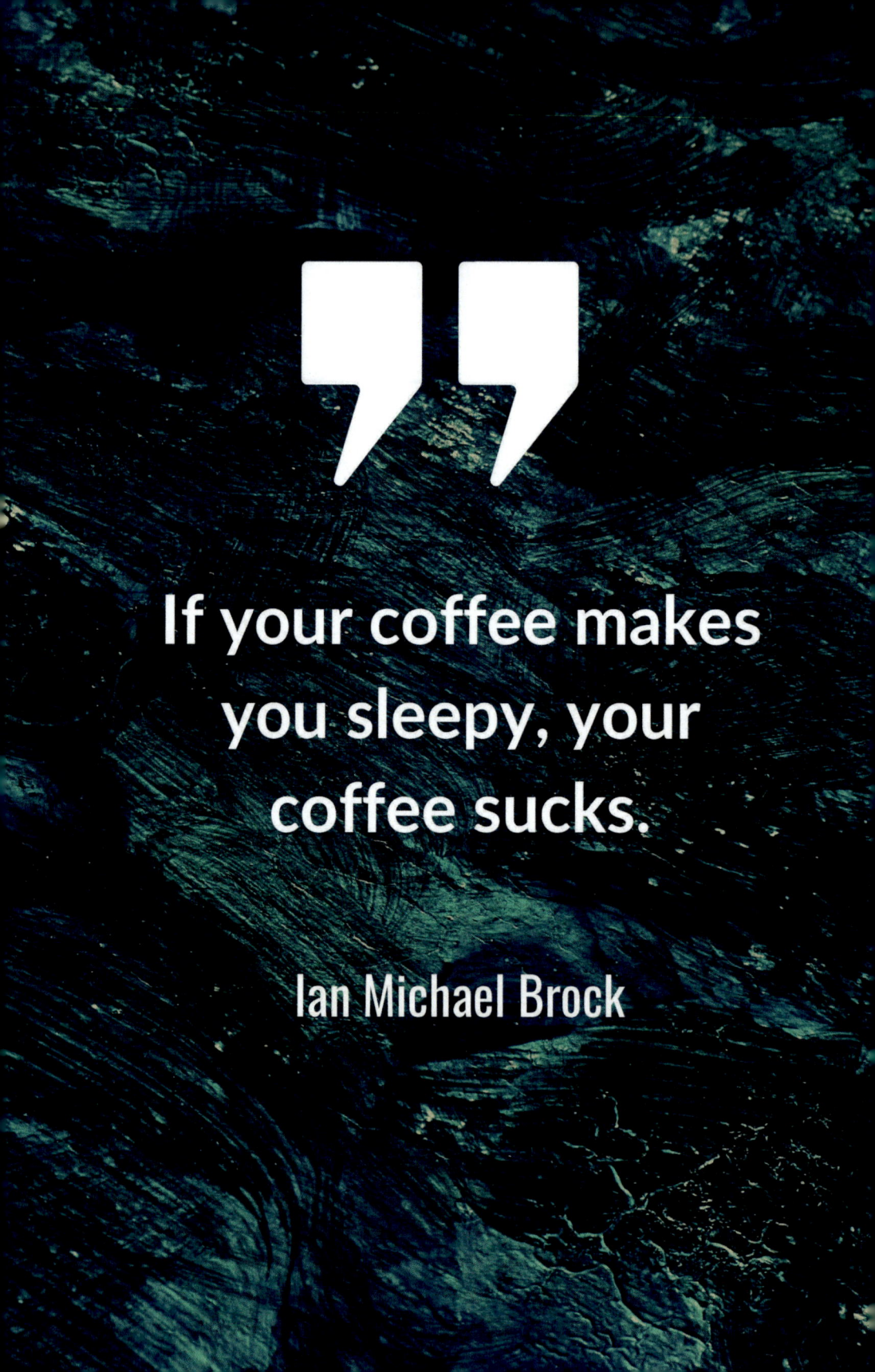

CHAPTER 9

Execution! When to Buy & When to Sell

So you did all the prep work in the beginning to set yourself up for success.

Now it's time to finish strong. The last part is knowing when to buy and sell your stock.

You should be able to look at a stock chart and know within 2 minutes where you want to get in and get out.

Here are some basics that can help you.

There's a ton of of strategies you can use to help you find out when to buy. One of those strategies is called **Dollar Cost Averaging (DCA)**.

In this strategy, you invest a certain amount on a regular basis (daily, weekly, monthly, quarterly, etc.) no matter what the stock price is.

DCA helps you buy stocks over time without thinking too much and looking at charts all day.

If you invested $200 a month, over one year, you would have invested $2,400!

If you add compound interest to that, you can make EVEN MORE money. I won't get into that in this book.

Simply put, if you reinvest your profits, the longer you wait the faster your money grows.

Now DCA only works on good companies that continue to grow.

If the company you picked is consistently going down, YOU WILL LOSE YOUR MONEY!

Buying and Selling

Another strategy to know when to buy is using INDICATORS. Indicators can help you predict where the price is going and when you should put your money in. One of the most popular indicators is the moving average (MA).

Here's how the moving average works. It takes the average price of a stock over a time frame and puts it onto a chart. The line moves in the same direction that the price is going. Since we're long-term investing, we want to use larger periods. Some popular ones you can use are the 50, 100, or 200-day averages.

If you watch sports, then you know each player has a stat keeping track of their average points each game. Think of a moving average as the company's points per game stats. It tells the story of how well they've done.

At this point, you're probably shaking your head and asking "How do we use this to know when to buy, Ian?"

That's easy and it's not as difficult as you think.

When the price of the stock is below the moving average line, you should think about going shopping. This tells us that the price is at a discount. You know we love savings around here so It's time to buy!

There are many different indicators out there, **BUT ONLY USE ONE**!

If you have too many of them on your chart, it will start to look like a 3 year old's drawing. We want to keep things simple.

I made this mistake before and it got me nowhere. It had me questioning my life decisions. Learn from my mistakes.

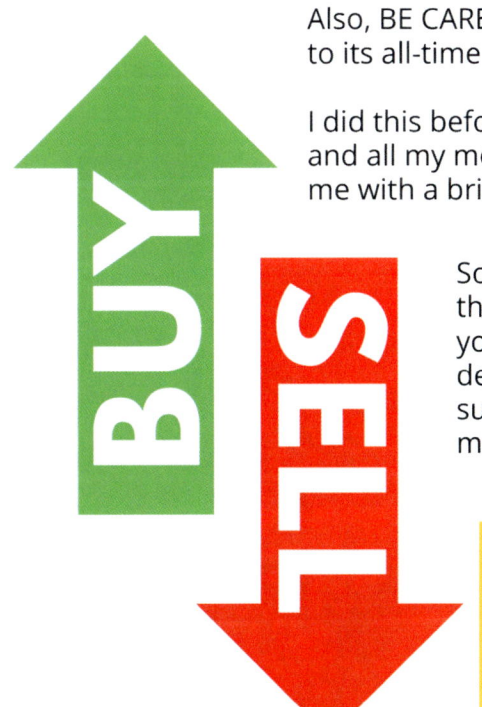

Also, BE CAREFUL investing in a stock that is close to its all-time high!

I did this before, and when I saw the price drop and all my money gone, it felt like someone hit me with a brick.

So if you hear people talk about it in the barbershop, hair salon, or school, you're probably too late. If you do decide to invest in the company, make sure they have plenty of room to make more money and grow.

TIP: A bonus indicator that I use is the **Fibonacci Retracement**. Before using it, do some research on how it works. I like using this one since it shows you different place you could buy and sell without doing too much work.

YESSIRSKIII. Now to the most exciting part, **knowing when to sell so you can make some money**!

There are two ways you can sell:

> - Sell at a **specific price**, or
> - Sell at a **specific time**

This all depends on what your goals are.

If you want to hold for the long term, you can hold for 5, 10, or even 20 years.

If you want to make a certain amount, pick how much you want to profit first. Do you want to make 20%, 50%, or 100% profit?

If you end up doubling your money, you should probably be looking to sell some of your stock and take profit. You don't have to sell all of your shares, just some.

Remember, being greedy can cause you to lose money if you wait too long to sell.

Once you choose your exit strategy, be patient and wait until you hit your target before selling.

WHERE TO BUY

Buying stocks is not as difficult as you might think.

If you like using your phone, you can use Cash App. This was the first app I used to buy my first stocks. Other good apps you can use are Webull and Robinhood.

If you're an advanced investor or someone who wants to learn more, you can invest using brokers like E*TRADE or TD Ameritrade. Using brokers can be more difficult but you do get access to all the advanced tools to invest in the market.

Boom, now you have the beginner's step-by-step plan to invest in stocks.

In case you forget, here are some resources you can use to do research:

StockAnalysis.com
to research different companies

TradingView.com
to look at charts and do technical analysis

CashApp
to buy stocks (Easy)

Robinhood & Webull
to buy stocks (Intermediate)

E*TRADE & TD Ameritrade Broker
to buy stocks (Advanced)

Now, it's time to apply what you learned. You now have the blueprint to become great at this.

I personally invested thousands of dollars into the market, with nothing but hopes and prayers. But hoping something works and prayer without action, doesn't get you very far.

I ended up losing 80% of that money because I wasn't prepared!

Practice these strategies until you become good at making investments. I don't want you to go through what I went through. Losing your hard earned money feels worse than getting kicked in the face.

Trust me, I know because both have happened to me before.

100 HOURS
So go out there and practice.

Spend at least 100 hours studying and preparing before you put a single cent in the market. You should become so good that you can look at a chart and know what price you want to buy and sell in under 30 seconds.

Professional athletes spend thousands of hours in the gym working on their craft. They get paid millions of dollars to be the best at what they do. If they're practicing that much as pros, shouldn't we do the same?

Now, take what you've learned from this chapter, and apply it!

START WHERE YOU ARE

CHAPTER 10

Crypto Currency

Oh my goodness, we are now in the endgame.

Welcome to the grand finale.

It's been a journey and if you've made it this far, congratulations!

We've all heard about Crypto Currency, NFTs, and the whole Web 3.0 world. But it's all just STUFF. There's so much information out there and honestly, it can be super confusing.

So in this chapter, we're going to cover the basics of Web 3.0.

I won't be showing you how to make money in it. That'll be for a different book.

If you are going to put money into this, PLEASE do your RESEARCH and educate yourself first.

I made the mistake of not doing that and lost thousands of dollars. I know others who lost almost $20,000 in this space.

Learn from our mistakes and do your research before you put a cent into crypto!

THE BEGINNING

The crypto universe all started from this thing called the **blockchain**.

All the blockchain does is securely save information. Whether it's info on people buying and selling things or anything else. Think of it as a "record book" that everyone in the world can see.

Whenever someone writes in this book, it creates a block. Each block connects with the last one, creating a chain of information. That's why it's called blockchain. Once someone writes in this "book," it can never be changed or erased.

Since everyone can see what's on these blocks, no one person is in control of the information. This is called decentralization (I know - it's a big word).

DECENTRALIZATION

Decentralization is when power and control is given to many people instead of one person who is in full control. Imagine a group project where everyone has an equal say and responsibility instead of one person making all the decisions. The opposite of this is Centralized, which means one person controls everything. Your teacher, for example, has complete control on what grades you get in class. If for some reason they don't like you and want to see you fail, they could change your grade to an F.

CRYPTOCURRENCY

All of this led to the creation of cryptocurrency. Crypto is digital money that only exists online. Think of it as an online payment system. Anyone can send or receive payments without using a bank.

Bitcoin is the most popular crypto out there and was the first one ever created. Some people even call it digital gold.

Every time someone moves around Bitcoin (buys or sells), it's recorded on the Bitcoin Blockchain. This makes it easier to track where everything is and makes it harder to commit fraud.

BUYING CRYPTO

Now if you want to buy crypto there's only 1 place you should go. That place is a crypto Exchange. Exchanges are just stores where you can buy and sell crypto easily. If you are buying Bitcoin, it's as easy as buying it on CashApp.

Unfortunately, if you want to buy other cryptos like Ethereum, you have to purchase them on exchanges. A few good exchanges are Binance and Coinbase. The only problem is, they have a lot of fees. If you want to save money on fees, you can use Coinbase Advance. It will save you up to 3% on fees and over time that adds up.

Coinbase Advance can be more complicated for beginners to use. But once you understand the platform it saves you a ton of money! Investing in crypto can feel exciting, but there are risks that come with it.

Unlike stocks, crypto prices move very fast and they can go up and down in an instant. This could lead to you losing most or even all of your money if you don't know what you're doing.

Some of the same principles you use to invest in stocks, you can use in crypto. You just have to practice as much as you can before you start investing!

NFTs

You might have heard of NFTs (Non-Fungible Tokens) like Bored Ape Yacht Club or all the other ones that were created in the past. Some of you might think that it's just a picture online, but it's more than that.

When you go to the grocery store and buy food, what do you get at the end? A receipt! That receipt lists everything that you bought, how much you spent, and that you are now the owner.

An NFT works the same way.

Think of an NFT as a receipt - it's just a way to verify that you purchased something and own it.

When you buy an NFT, some type of product comes with it. This is called the **Utility**.

Think of the **utility as the value behind that NFT**. Without that value, it's worthless.

In the future, you may buy an NFT that includes concert tickets. Those tickets are the **utility** and give that NFT Value. You aren't paying for just the NFT. Nobody cares about a worthless picture. You're buying the item that comes with it, which in this case is the concert tickets.

The beautiful part is that, every NFT is unique so there can never be duplicates.

Nobody can ever be sold a fake copy of something which is a good thing for us non-scammers.

NFTs have unlimited potential for how they can be used.

The most powerful tool that they have is the **royalty fees**. A creator of an NFT can set a certain percentage they make every time it's resold.

Through NFTs, new artists can make money from their albums years after they release them.

All they have to do is set their royalty percentage. Once their music blows up years later, artists can still make money every time their work is resold. This gives creators a new way to make money from their art.

Also, NFTs could make it much easier to buy real world items. If you've ever purchased a house before, you know that it could take weeks or even months before you move in. The whole process can take forever.

But with NFTs you could buy one much faster with fewer closing fees.

In February 2022, someone in Florida bought a house using an NFT for $654,000. Now imagine a world where everything you purchase comes with an NFT, verifying that you are the real owner of that item.

No one can ever claim your stuff and steal it from you since you own the NFT!

SECURITY

BOOM! You are now a CRYPTO EXPERT! Well not really, but you know a whole lot more about this space than the average person.

Now it's time to protect your assets from being stolen from you. The best way to keep your crypto and NFTs safe is to use a crypto wallet.

Think of a crypto wallet as a digital safe that helps you store and manage your assets. There are two types of Wallets: a Hot wallet and a Cold wallet.

A **hot wallet** is connected to the internet which makes it easy to access. Some hot wallets are MetaMask, Coinbase Wallet, and Trust Wallet, which are all free.

They make it easy to buy and sell your items online. The only risk is that someone can hack into your wallet and steal all your crypto since it's connected to the internet.

But **cold wallets** are much safer and are perfect for storing large amounts of crypto and NFTs.

Cold wallets are actual devices about the size of a thumb drive. It's literally a hard drive for your crypto that you connect to your computer or phone to make transactions. Some cold wallets include the Ledger Nano X and the Trezor wallets.

Here's the thing, they are expensive. You can spend up to $150 for one. But, if you plan on spending thousands on crypto, I would suggest you buy a cold wallet so you can keep your items safe.

PURCHASE CRYPTO FROM TRUSTED SITES

On top of all that, we must ONLY buy crypto from trusted sites.

It's like buying a pair of Jordans from a guy off of Ebay or going to a place like GOAT to get them. You might get scammed on Ebay but since GOAT is a verified shoe store, it's less likely to happen there.

Make sure that you're buying crypto from verified exchanges ONLY.

Also, stay on the top 3 platforms. There have been scandals in the past where some exchanges took advantage of people by taking their money. The rankings of the top 3 will change over time so just do a quick search on which are the best and safest.

WATCH OUT FOR SCAMS

And then of course WATCH OUT for scams.

People will try to convince you to buy their new "Crypto." Some will even beg you to give them money so they can invest for you. THEY'RE ALL FAKE! I knew a person who was told that if they gave someone $10,000, they could turn that money into $500k. They sent the scammer their money and never saw it again.

So If it's too good to be true . . . then it probably is.

MOST IMPORTANTLY

PLEASE NEVER SHARE YOUR PERSONAL DATA!
NEVER SHARE your private crypto keys, your passwords, or your personal data. As smart, beautiful people with great elbows, you already have experienced this with the internet. So the same applies with crypto.

RESOURCES

Just in case you forgot, here are the resources you can use on your journey into crypto.

01 **CoinMarketCap.com**
Use to research all cryptos and look at the overall crypto market

02 **Coinbase.com / Coinbase Advanced**
This is an Exchange where you buy and sell crypto

03 **Binance**
This is another Exchange where you buy and sell crypto

04 **MetaMask**
This is a hot wallet that allows you to save your crypto and NFTs while still being connected online

05 **Coinbase Wallet**
This is a hot wallet that allows you to save your crypto and NFTs while still being connected online

My beautiful people, we are at the end of this chapter!

What a journey! I hope this brought a lot of value to you.

Although we didn't talk about ways to make money in crypto, it's important that you first understand how it works.

Use this information to start your journey into the Web 3.0 world. There are so many creative ways you can use Web 3.0 in your lives, now it's time for you to discover them. Apply what you learned in this chapter so you can win more and lose less!

> "If you don't like the output, change your input."
>
> — Myron Golden

CHAPTER 11

Taxes

JUST PAY YOUR TAXES

IT'S THAT SIMPE!

If you need help filing your taxes, go to H&R Block, TurboTax or any other tax prep company to get started.

> If you can't fly, then run. If you can't run, then walk. If you can't walk, then crawl, but whatever you do, you have to keep moving.

MARTIN LUTHER KING JR.

CHAPTER 12

Conclusion - The End

Wow, what a journey. I'm at a loss for words right now.

I'm so proud of you for making it this far. You did that!

Give yourself a pat on the back, and go treat yourself to something nice because you deserve it.

I truly do appreciate you for reading until the end. It means the world that you trust me enough to share this knowledge and information with you.

It took years of research, testing, and firsthand experience to find all of this.

I hope you found this book valuable and that it changed your money mindset. I hope that you now believe that your dream life is just a few steps away!

Bruce Lee once said "**Knowing is not enough we must APPLY. Willing is not enough, we must DO.**"

With all the knowledge in this book, it doesn't matter if you memorized everything and took notes, if you don't apply what you learned.

My final task for you is to take everything you learned and put it into ACTION!

Create something with it! Go out there and be GREAT!

I wrote this book as a guide and it's now up to you to start and **bend reality to your will**.

You were born to do amazing things.

The fact that you made it to the end of this book is a sign that you are ready!

Don't worry about what others have to say.

Don't worry about succeeding or failing. You got this.

So go out there and create the life that you were meant to live!

Made in the USA
Coppell, TX
23 September 2024